# CHEETAHS
# GUEPARDOS

Amelie von Zumbusch

Traducción al español: Ma. Pilar Sanz

**PowerKiDS** press™ & **Editorial Buenas Letras**™

New York

Published in 2007 by The Rosen Publishing Group, Inc.
29 East 21st Street, New York, NY 10010

First Edition

Book Design: Erica Clendening
Layout Design: Julio Gil and Lissette González

Photo Credits: Cover, pp. 1, 9, 11, 17, 19, 23, 24 (top left, top right, bottom right) © Digital Vision; p. 5 © Artville; pp. 7, 13, 15, 21, 24 (bottom left) © Digital Stock.

Cataloging Data

Zumbusch, Amelie von.
  Cheetahs-Guepardos / by Amelie von Zumbusch: traducción al español Ma. Pilar Sanz — 1st ed.
      p. cm. — (Safari animals-Animales de safari)
  Includes bibliographical references and index.
  ISBN-13: 978-1-4042-7604-8 (library binding)
  ISBN-10: 1-4042-7604-1 (library binding)
  1. Cheetah—Juvenile literature. 2. Spanish language materials I. Title.

Manufactured in the United States of America

# CONTENTS

# CONTENIDO

Cheetahs are members of the cat family. They sometimes purr as house cats do.

---

Los guepardos pertenecen a la familia de los gatos. Algunas veces, los guepardos ronronean como los gatos.

5

The cheetah is the fastest animal on Earth. Cheetahs can run as fast as 70 miles per hour (113 km/hr).

---

El guepardo es el animal más rápido sobre la Tierra. Los guepardos pueden correr hasta 70 millas por hora (113 km/hr).

A cheetah's coat is covered with black spots. Cheetahs have a black stripe on each side of their nose.

---

El pelaje de los guepardos tiene manchas negras. Los guepardos tienen una raya negra a cada lado de la nariz.

9

Cheetahs have small heads and thin bodies. This helps them run fast.

---

Los guepardos tienen la cabeza pequeña y el cuerpo muy delgado. Esto los ayuda a correr rápido.

Most cheetahs live on the savannahs of Africa.

---

La mayoría de los guepardos viven en la sabana africana.

13

Cheetahs eat meat. They run fast to catch animals for food.

---

Los guepardos comen carne. Los guepardos corren rápido para atrapar a otros animales.

Many cheetahs live alone. Others live in small family groups.

---

Algunos guepardos viven solos. Otros guepardos viven en familia, en grupos pequeños.

Cheetah cubs are born with gray fur on their backs. They get spots when they are a few months old.

---

Los cachorros de guepardo nacen con pelaje gris en la espalda. Después de algunos meses les salen manchas negras.

19

Young cheetahs live with their mothers until they are between one and two years old.

---

Los guepardos viven con sus mamás hasta que cumplen uno o dos años.

There are not many cheetahs left in the wild. There are some parks where they can live safely, though.

---

No quedan muchos guepardos en la sabana. Algunos guepardos viven protegidos en parques y zoológicos.

23

# Words to Know / Palabras que debes saber

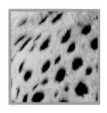

coat / (el) pelaje

cubs / (los) cachorros

savannah / (la) sabana

stripe / (la) raya